WORKING CLASS VOODOO

Working Class Voodoo

BOBBY PARKER

FOR NICKI

WITH LOVE AND
ADMIRATION

THANK YOU FOR
BEING AMAZING! X

[signature]

3. 5. 18

First published in 2018
by Offord Road Books

www.offordroadbooks.co.uk
@OffordRoadBooks

Typeset by Offord Road Books
Printed in the UK by TJ International

ISBN 978–1–999–93041–7

1 3 5 7 9 10 8 6 4 2

O•R•B

*for Katy
& Isobelle*

Contents

WORKING CLASS VOODOO

Fruit Machine

I withdraw my sickness
benefits from the Post Office
so excited
I could shit my pants.

Wetherspoons special
turkey dinner and craft beer
with a picture
of a tiger.

Everyone I love is asleep.
If they're not asleep
they wish
they were asleep.

I don't think about factories
in the snow
or what song my mum has
stuck in her head
when she's scraping
early morning
ice off the car.

I don't think about the time
my dad couldn't explain
he just sort of
shrieked
into my shoulder.

I feed warm banknotes
into the beer-sticky slot
until they're gone.

Later, I howl in your car.
Cold wind and rain.
Grey into grey
into grey.

My fingers
webbed with snot.
You beg me not to break
the passenger window
with my face.

Then you say
everything is going
to be okay, and that you love me
you love me
you love me
fruit machine
or no fruit machine.

Christ on a bike.

No one said
this
was going
to be beautiful
but, for some reason, it is.

King of Eggs

When we tried to quit
drinking
            again
I got so bored
I would throw eggs
onto the street
late at night
after the clubs had closed
they weren't rotten or anything
they were perfectly
good eggs
my usual target
was drunk lads
shouting awful things
at girls walking home alone
there was a tall fence
around our property
since I couldn't see
where my eggs landed
I aimed for voices
avoiding the odd passing car
hoping for a headshot
it gave me a silly buzz
and made Katy laugh
that's all I wanted
we rented a house with a big garden
there was a pond
surrounded by lawn ornaments
birds dogs and a small boy pissing

creepy in the moonlight
sometimes I felt quite mad
standing on the wet grass
with a cold egg
in each hand
watching
the neighbours' lights
go out
one by one
often the street was dead
but I threw eggs
           anyway
listening for the sound of them
smacking the pavement
so satisfying
like ice cracking
or popping the cork from a bottle
then I would go back in the house
to stare into the light
of the empty fridge
the way I stare
into open churches
           eventually
creeping upstairs to look down
from the bedroom window
at all the shattered shells
and glistening yolks
on the silent road
           astonished
by my work
and slightly
afraid.

Thank You For Swallowing My Cum

I tell cats on the street, 'Hey kitty, she swallowed my cum!'
I told the shy Indian woman in the corner shop, 'Do not be
    afraid,
for she swallowed my cum!' I even told my mum but she
burned her elbow on the frying pan, and then showed me
a pile of depressing bank statements as my dad blew a perfect
ring of smoke that broke like the ghost of a cheap wedding
band above the empty fruit bowl. While pissing into the sea
on a beautiful day in Barmouth last week, I cupped
my hands around my stoned smile and yelled, 'Hey sunset,
she swallowed my cum!' but it shrugged between misty hills
as the tide rolled over my shoes and my ex-wife hates me.
Or she sometimes hates me. And she never swallowed my cum.
What am I doing? Where am I going? Are you okay?
Can I get you anything? I won't swallow your cum
but I could make you a sandwich. I should probably
send her a message, make sure it's cool to share this
poem. I don't want to make her feel awkward;
awkward that I saw myself clean in her company, my blood
baptismal water; awkward that I saw myself happily dying
as her fingers scribbled sad stories onto my pale chest;
awkward that I tell cats, and nervous Indian women,
and my stressed parents, and amazing, horrible,
gore-porn sunsets that Oh Wow! when she swallowed
my cum I forgot how dead I am because when I'm living
inside her mouth I don't even need to breathe . . .

Binge-watching Bad Memories

Nothing sorts out memories from ordinary moments. It is only later that they claim remembrance, when they show their scars.

— CHRIS MARKER

congratulations your head didn't explode
in the supermarket
nothing triggered us
can you believe that
no one cares
I plant fists in my hair
squint a million oranges
touch myself with caution
convinced I'm an alien
tangled like earphones
fingers pulling at the knots
the hem of my red dress
I mean your red dress
whispering through the ashtray
talking to a nurse she said
you probably won't die tonight
we agreed
our feet were
equally disgusting
I peeled his hand off my knee
told him to go
wait for the dealer
he can remember
dancing but sometimes
he can't remember

the year she was born
shiver in a spoon
I rarely think about God
did you really see him
in the park
bumming a dog
behind a burned-out car
dirty old bastard
I heard he worked in a factory
making fences
your mother was struggling to breathe
your dad fell off a ladder
cleaning windows
on a hot day
you could drink
a frosty pint of beer
in 1.9 seconds
but that doesn't mean
anything to me now
it doesn't matter
what I think
we are all in a lot of pain
your dad is mowing the lawn
even though
it will be dark soon
I've never seen a person
mow the lawn
in the dark
so I'm obviously
quite excited
when I'm excited

I sniff my fingers
until it makes me feel weird
then I wash my hands
tonight they smell
sort of evil
just think of the fresh cut
grass on the bottom
of your dad's shoes
I can't seem to write my love for you
the pharmacist always
makes a joke of us
as we stare at mouthwash
waiting for pills
if I don't get these pills
I might have a seizure
if I have a seizure
maybe I will become a witness
if I can describe what I see
without prejudice
perhaps there will come a day
without prescriptions
organic shampoo
the colour of churches
waiting room chairs
with impressions of arses
I try on a pair of pink sunglasses
a young black woman
pleads with the pharmacist
her boyfriend beat her
with a Poundland brolly
next time he's gonna

fucking murder me
I rest the daft glasses on my lips
pretend I'm not listening
did you know
the fair is in town
it smells of skunk
win me a teddy
oh squeeze me on the ghost train
I'm sorry but Kidderminster
is terribly white
disgusting really
her boyfriend calls her a whore
even as he takes the money
she makes off these streets
no problem
he was my best friend
in high school
we did a lot of speed together
I thought he died
he should have died
the pharmacist
has very beautiful hands
she picks up the phone
as if she's the first person
to ever pick up a phone
my taxi waiting
between McDonald's
and the Job Centre
how long have I been here
I'm trying to remember
or trying to look

as though I'm trying
to remember
what happened to us
didn't we kiss
our mouths all chocolatey
like a million years ago
under a tree or something
flashing blue lights
standing over the sink
I cup my hands
under the boiling hot tap
until my fingers feel like saints
she sacrificed London
for my anxious hands
lightning for my jealousy
sexuality for my toothbrush
I said things that hurt her breasts
I said my chest is full of scarecrows
I said our bed is a famous ghost ship
She feels the true night
when I break my neck
to kiss her out of her bones
our home town was built
on *Sun* newspapers and tired mothers
standing crooked in their kitchens
waiting for the bats
it seems like everyone is somehow
involved with smack
nothing works
Spring by Antonio Vivaldi
tortured into a tin-can toy phone

by the Department of Work & Pensions
She tells me clouds are gay
just to watch me try to figure out
if it's going to rain
in my most submissive role
she sees a girl
with eyes that punish fathers
as a demon breeze
hisses through the corn
she sees a frightened boy
who in the aftermath
of childhood assaults
pulled women closer
told them everything
told them too much
made them wary
she honestly believed
I could read her mind
until the meds kicked in
now we have
repeat prescriptions
we stand around the same
mysterious body as you
cursing
death to the ice-cream man
death to the postman
death to the policeman
death to the fireman
death to the man who cuts the label off my shirt
death to this paltry allowance
death as my voice the same as your voice

death as her voice
disguised as my voice
disguised as strange thoughts
you're having right now
in our joyful coming
we are your noisiest neighbours
she searched under my bed
but didn't find a monster
perhaps you could try again later
our lines are busy
the cuts have been made
we taught our scars to flicker
our appeal is pending
through the poisoned city
I wish to make a new claim
my mouth
just like your mouth
is only the beginning
and I don't know how long
he tortured me for
I don't remember what he did
only that I was sweaty
from screaming for mum and dad
to come home
pay him for babysitting
get rid of him
call the fucking police
help me
whenever I smell burning toast
I remember that's what he offered
in return for silence

carefully holding the plate up
to the top bunk
where I shivered like a puppy
the pain was mine
sleep could not touch it
the victim heat
of guilt and shame was endless
I got used to it
you do
don't you
I would stare straight at the sun
I set dead trees on fire
abandoned buildings
my own soiled underwear
in the gallery of evil penises
my childhood neighbour's
is definitely in the top three
greyish
slimy
reeked of cheese
five years later
he became the first heroin addict I knew
vomiting his stomach lining
outside our local newsagents
then he hanged himself
before any of this I remember
mum shouting for me
her pink fingers dripping
dish suds on the doorstep
where are you
I'm so sorry

I sleep too much
I'm not so ugly when I'm asleep
I can't hear my ex-wife crying
or her junkie boyfriend
yelling at my daughter
I can still feel the breath
of confused boys in my ear
hot tears in the soft eye
of a sad dad's moon
when my daughter
stays with her mother
I eat all the turkey dinosaurs
finish the blackcurrant
squash by her bed
scrape off the bright blue toothpaste
she spits on the edge of the sink
sometimes I get up
in middle of the night
to sleep in her empty pink bed
and I still dream
that I'm way up in the sky
during a terrifying storm
atop a 20-foot wooden pole
that's been shoved up my ass
and I'm clenching
my sphincter
with all my strength
so it won't go all the way
up through my guts
and out the top of my head
thank goodness for the tablets we take

right
on the inside
we must look like
candy factories
colour dissolving
blood glittering as the heart
sees its own blue ghost
and shudders.

Edible Ghosts

Yesterday was the hottest day
in the history of the world,
everybody died
and came back to life
and then died again
and now we're waiting
for the pizza delivery man
to call to say he cannot find us.
When I carry the tall fan
from the living room to the bedroom
I like to pretend I'm Jesus.
Katy says my ass looks good
in these yellow pants
and it's my turn
to take the rubbish out.
The kitchen is full of broken glass,
this wouldn't be a problem
if I could stop thinking about blood –
some nights I can't keep an erection
for the image of her
silent-screaming
in a salmon-coloured armchair.
There have been three burglaries
in the last couple of weeks,
when they hit the restaurant
across the street
they took everything
even the vegetables.
I watch the family downstairs

water plants around the building.
They are waiting for the police.
The man is slowly winding
a garden hose around his arm,
his grey ponytail upsets me.
The woman is sitting
on a wall, chain-smoking,
I drink her patient smile.
Their little girl shrieks with joy,
soaked to the skin on a purple scooter.
I wish her happiness
didn't bug me so much.
There must be 1,000 photos
of my daughter on my phone.
I look at them every day and feel
pain like the discovery
of a new planet.
She is approximately 131.9 miles away.
Text message from mother asks
if I sold any paintings yet
sold any books yet
and you know
you can't come home.
Katy begs me to destroy the drugs
I've been holding for old times' sake.
I've been stalling for 22 minutes.
When I give her the pills
she crushes the silver
packet in her fist, runs to the bathroom
and flushes them.
After, we cry.

I'm not even supposed to be alive.
I want to tell you
that London anxiety
is Pac-Man Biblical
but I don't even know
what that means.
The hipsters are partying
in the opposite building,
they
laugh
laugh
laugh.
An old black woman stops
to lean on their gate, her exhausted
eyes approximately
99% more human,
shopping bags
like storm clouds on the kerb.
A film is playing on Netflix,
the subtitles read:
'I also know
how important
it is in life
not necessarily to be strong
but to feel strong.'
If it thunders
hard tonight
with union lightning
strikes over the bulging city
and her sad little car
I'm certain all of this

will mean something.
Meanwhile, the newsagent
is open until 3 a.m.
I'm getting beer fat again
and we have developed
a loving bond
with the otherness
of lamps.

Fat Girls

First there was Overweight Haters
handing out malicious
fat-shaming cards
on the Tube
now there's this morning's article
in a popular magazine
that says men
attracted to fat girls
are considered to be deviants
with low self-confidence
it says fat girls
often experience
intense shame
on behalf of their partners
& the beautiful world
basically hates them
I guess you haven't thought about it before
maybe you didn't want to think about it
staring at your hands
they seem broken & far away
as if a tired mother
bandaged them in the dark
you hope she doesn't think
this is why you haven't introduced her
to your parents
you grab your soft belly with both hands
shaking & squeezing
until it's red in the mirror
& while she sleeps

drunk dreaming
pure & sad
as the next person
& every other person
in the beach-body world
you imagine all of us
swimming deep underwater
where bombs sleep
& monsters cry
everybody diving
until our drowned hearts sing
a history of clouds
away from the weight of weight
away from the size of size
screaming bubbles
death gone mad
skin for the wasted angels
& as we break
laughing
blood free
into the clean white light
of knowing for sure
love will be
slow & strange again
you will not care
it will fit anywhere
a sweet woozy god of a thing
you knock empty bottles
spinning sideways
into the sun
as you leap out of bed

dragging the covers behind you
to stand
squinting at her
fat
naked
body
– which is right –
as if something is wrong
& you're trying to see it
you're trying to see it
but you can't.

Ginger

I ask her to turn me into a pretty girl,
not drag for laughs like Jimmy
whose whisky makes me gag.

His frightened wig
the candyfloss of demons.

She empties her make-up bag
on the floor, a bird's-eye
view of the fair.

I kneel between the brushes
and summon her American lovers,
tongues too big for their mouths.

A boy with shivering
hazel eyes and hands that flicker
says he snorted nine bags of meow
when the horses were asleep.

He says I have good skin
but he does not dance.

Queer! barks my father's voice
through powder
palpitations.

Her smile as she works
is a special kind of weather
reserved for the tops of mountains.

I'm convinced she will leave me for a girl.
She says she doesn't want to be with a girl.
She is turning me into a pretty girl.

Look up, that's right.
Open your mouth, that's good.
Now press your lips together.

The heart is fast.
The night is church.
Jimmy's drugs were cut with sugar.

/

(Backslash, from the Asterism *anthology of punctuation)*

These days the best times
are when I'm walking with my daughter
holding her warm little hand
picking flowers
or talking about what we see in the clouds
I tell myself that our hands
holding each other
is the beginning and the end of the universe
I experience everything
the past present and future
from the perspective of our hands
and I don't want to let go
I bite my tongue hard so I don't cry in front of her
our hands are the only real thing
I have left
letting go of my daughter's hand
when it's time for her to go home
hurts more than I ever thought it possible to hurt
it always feels like the last time
I hate letting go of my daughter's hand
I hope she never grows out of holding my hand
please baby always hold my hand
I carry a lock of hair from her first haircut
blonde in a clear bag in a silver tin
if I don't have that silver tin with me I get very anxious
I have given my girlfriend strict instructions
to put my daughter's hair into my hand

should something happen
a strange hospital somewhere
a bed that smells of other medicated people
in a medicated nightmare they couldn't wake up from
more doctors and more drugs and more of this
not feeling anything
really
just not being much of a problem
for anybody anymore because I'm so drugged
thank you doctor
this has been a great help I think
what do you think
of course I will get over this
I hope I get over this
because I have love
doesn't stop it from being fucking terrifying
almost all of the time
look at my eyes they are frightened eyes
I've been called a wounded deer
I've been called a pussy
I've been called inside out away from God
I don't care
I want to care
my psychiatrist looked into my eyes and smiled
she said I have just the thing for you
I told her my daughter's name
but she wasn't listening
she was searching through a book for a drug
she seemed so satisfied with the word quetiapine
Queeeee Tiaaaa Peeeen
I told her my daughter's name again

but she didn't care
or she didn't hear me
or she didn't understand
she prodded the page with a crooked old finger
she said I want you to try this drug it's called
Queeeee Tiaaaa Peeeeeeeen
the drippy cartoons
at the end of my arms
flying
for the sun the moon the stars in the room
Isobelle I cried Isobelle it's Isobelle

Silver Thumbs

It's got nothing to do with you, she says.
Her boyfriend shouting in the background.
The father of her next child.
I'm the master of shitty messages.
I hang up and think about silver thumbs
hailing benefits in the town hall,
their tracksuit pockets
full of folded scratchcards.
I think about my doctor
washing his hands
a hundred times a day
telling me I need to stop obsessing.
My daughter runs into my arms,
I tell her clouds change shape for us.
She wanted a little sister.
I tell her not to be sad,
there's a million colouring books out there
and daddy bought a kitten.
When I heard the news I watched clips
from *Rosemary's Baby* and ate
too many chocolate eggs.
Now I stare at bins along the street
and think about her house,
which is forgetting us, it has
already started to move.
A burned-out car on the lawn,
bonnet open with a dirty engine
laughing at the sun.
Social Services

straight to answerphone.
Her stepdad's head with horns.
My fake blood
tricks flies into believing
someone died instead of being born.

Working Class Voodoo

This is me holding a voodoo doll.
This is me waving the doll over the hob.
This is me being silly, doll down my pants,
shrugging like a nineties sitcom doofus.
This is also me, going a bit mad, in the garden.
Ha-ha . . . Look at the sky! Weird isn't it?
That's my dear old mum, bless her, screaming.
Without her my daughter wouldn't have nice clothes.
There's dad, half cut, staring at a black cloth.
We never came to blows and I'm proud of that.
They're always asking what happened, oh
what happened, son, what happened?
The voodoo doll is not meant to represent
anyone in particular, although I'm sure
you're sharp enough to notice it bears
a striking resemblance to the snake man
who rattles beside my wife and sells
her telly for dope; who sometimes tells
my daughter to wipe herself on a towel
because they can't afford toilet paper;
who isn't bothered the divorce isn't fixed yet.
We are talking about the biggest creep in town,
living with my daughter, doing heroin
next to the bedroom where she wets herself.
I could kill him I could kill him I could.
Anyway, this is me throwing the doll
as far as I can, then running after it
on all fours with the most beautiful sunset
exploding cake and bottles of pink wine.

I mean clean powder and a holy syringe.
I mean glory, glory, my girlfriend's smile.
Finally, this is me in my doctor's office.
She wants to increase the medication,
thinks it will improve my quality of life.
She says perhaps it's not that I left a home,
or that I left a wife & child, it's because
I walked away from love, and those of us
who walk away from love are haunted
and we must learn to live again, bound
by the rules of the haunted cult of walking away.
You know, I wrote a poem about how much I hate
our abusive neighbours, just before it was published
they mysteriously moved out. Isn't that spooky?
And my wife looks at me like I fucking murdered her.
And her boyfriend smokes it he doesn't inject!
And my daughter kisses the freckles on my arm.
She says, 'Why did you leave us daddy?'
She tells me their budgies die from hunger.
She says daddy is so forgetful, his brain must be
a half-crushed sandcastle, waiting for the sea.
Then there's this doll, posing for a photograph.
This is me holding a match and a can of petrol.
The truth I beg you the truth the truth the truth.
Haunted for the haunted for the haunted forever.
I sometimes wonder if I wrote a broken family
into existence, using poems like this, and that
someday, maybe, I could write them back.

Tiny Skulls

It's Friday night and the monster between the trees
leans closer, sniffs our pain, laughs a hundred fireworks.
We listen to drunk neighbours through the dividing
    chimney,
they hate me because I don't go to work in a factory.
'I work seventy hours a week!' he screeches at his family,
and when he stumbles down the garden path I'm slumped
by the pond, staring at my hands, heavily medicated.
His kids call him an evil pig, his wife sobs when he drinks,
sometimes it sounds like he's pulling his house apart
brick by brick and screaming that it's all because of me.
I imagine his head is full of machines machines machines.
I guess I'm rubbing it in somehow, with my pill box
    shuffle,
sunglasses on the wonk, watching ants for hours.
When the police take him away I wonder why it matters.
His yellow work van like a giant crayon in the rain.
His wife's car like a donor kidney by the black bins.
The sad sounds they make through the dividing chimney,
the foul smell that drifts out of the dividing chimney
like a demonic presence, late at night, when we're
    spooked.
I tell Katy I'm certain her parents hate me for the same
reasons our neighbours hate me, and my folks
disappointed as ghosts, chanting work work work, boy!
My GP swivels to face the trainee nurse, he says: 'Bobby
is a recovering addict, bipolar, struggling to fill the void.'
He sends me away with tiny skulls in silver packets.
Most of the time I tell people I'm doing my own thing,
which means benefits, I'm afraid to say I'm on benefits,

coffin head, dancing manic dirt magic benefits,
medicine leaflets, side effects, a life sawn in half
by benefits and the so-called happiness they bring
to sofas, spliffs, broken beds, frozen pizzas;
a vision of myself hanging in the attic as the dividing
chimney sighs seventy years of dole dust: get a job,
if you can't get a job at least pretend to go somewhere,
leave the house with purpose, wear stinky trainers,
kick your mental illness like a muddy football,
like a pile of empty Coke cans, like the stupid dog
that it is, shitting all over the house, barking
all night long because it doesn't know anything
except for barking all night long at the beautiful
benefits of worried love; the beautiful benefits
of the dividing chimney, the way sound gets
all screwed up in the dividing chimney: I can hear
the man next door calling me a cunt because I don't
work in a factory, his voice like scrambled eggs, his wife
begging him to go to bed please go to bed I'm scared.
It matters so much to him, it matters so much
to her parents and my parents and the local newspaper
with depressed men's bodies dragged from canals,
pig heads and trotters tossed on Muslim lawns,
food banks, blood banks, car crash, cheeky wanks,
stabbings in the park where my daughter picks flowers,
dealers on the corner where the sun dips down and out,
every window is a bloody cross on a white flag
and everyone is telling us to leave, telling us to work
in a factory for seventy hours a week, our neighbours
hiding in the dividing chimney, plotting, breathing
old soot, calling us faggots, freaks, desperate in darkness,
whispering: 'Shut the fuck up, it's time to light the fire.'

Schnook

We found a house in a low crime area.
In fact zero crimes, according to online stats.
I wonder how that's possible in this town
where even the statues are 'gouging out'.
It's the perfect home, close to Isobelle's school
with an alleyway at the end of the street
that leads straight into town. Immaculate
lawns, posh cars, and the silence of living
at the edge of the countryside. Honestly,
I don't know how we ended up here.
Maybe, after spending so long living
in rough areas surrounded by fucked up
people and the victims of government cuts,
we have come to earn this wonderful place.
After battling addiction my whole life
and overcoming it, maybe I have earned
this position among the beautifully mundane.
Lucky not to be dead or in jail.
I will get up early and do the housework.
I will cook fresh food and tend the garden.
I will bake treats for our new neighbours
since we have always been on bad terms
with the horrible families here, who beat
their wives and kids who scream
and scream and scream. Yessiree bob.
No action. No drama. Gone the sirens
that nip our nerves out here between
the hospital and the police station. Gone
the days of scoring, using, scoring, waiting,

rattling, running, dying, fighting, using, falling,
loaning, lying, cheating, scoring, quitting,
rattling, relapsing, over and over again
in the rain. Looking at our new house
on this quiet street where nothing happens
I think of the last lines from the film
Goodfellas: 'I'm an average nobody . . .
Get to live the rest of my life like a schnook.'
Except it's a good thing. I mean, it's amazing
leaving that life. Right? I won't miss it at all.

Piñata

We were looking for a cat litter tray
in the pet department
of a local superstore
when I had this awful feeling
of not knowing
who you are
and what we are doing
together.
The smell of dog treats
made me queasy.
I stopped to watch an advert
for cat toys on a small screen
above the fluffy mice.
The assistant manager
lingered nearby, I recognised him
from high school art class.
He has five children
with a much older woman.
This terrified me for some reason.
I hid behind a crate of birdseed
wondering what it must be like
to have five children
with a much older woman
and not recognise
any of them.
You smiled at me and held my hand.
A sense of familiarity flickered
through this depression,
I recognised you

and we made our way to the exit.
In the car, everything seemed okay.
We stopped at a petrol station.
I watched you fill the tank
and loved you so much
I thought the car would explode.
Later, my mum popped in for tea.
You were talking about party food
for Isobelle's birthday.
I didn't recognise my mum
as fully as I used to.
Navy blue factory uniform,
and steel toecap boots
and no time
for mental illness.
Mum said she'd make sandwiches.
You said that sounds great.
I sat perfectly still in the kitchen,
watching you both,
petrified of my brain.
When she left you picked up
the piñata you made last night
and filled it with sweets,
rubber dinosaurs and confetti.
I could still smell cat piss
even though we bought
a more expensive litter box
with a roof and a door
to contain the odour.

Swine

The taxi driver told me
about the post-Brexit pigs' heads
left in his Muslim neighbour's garden.
Jeez, I said. That's fucking disgusting.
Oh it wasn't just the one, he said.
More like nine or ten.
It started with arguments
over parking spaces.
Then there was rotting pigs' trotters
hanging from door handles
and dark blood splashed up the walls.
I grew up with these people, he said.
They're sound, never bother anyone
and I get takeaways half price.
He pointed to the pile of rubble
where the leisure centre used to be.
See that? he said, turning the meter off.
Apparently it's gonna be a mosque.
The other one's too small now,
kids keep vandalising it.
I tried to picture this new mosque
with the notorious Lion Hotel
just down the street – its pale, angry
smackheads with tattered England flags
waving from their cracked windows.
Poverty. Wankers. Women screaming.
Yeah, he said, it's a shame what's happening
but it doesn't surprise me.
I took off my sunglasses and rubbed them

with the bottom of my white shirt
trying to think of something to say.
Where did they get all them heads from?
I mean, ten pigs' heads is quite a lot,
don't you think?
But he couldn't hear me
over the sudden boom of taxi jargon
crackling out the speakers
as he stopped opposite my house
and started counting change
out of an old plastic lunch box
he kept under his seat.

Nothing Scary

After we broke up
she gave me a slice
of birthday cake
she baked for herself.

A simple jam sponge
dusted with icing sugar.

I didn't want to eat it
or throw it away
– both felt wrong –
so I kept it
in a clear plastic tub
in my parents' shed.

Three years later
the cake is still there
behind the lawnmower
worshipped by spiders.
Still sort of fresh-looking
and saintly in that tub.

I have considered
various moonlight rituals
most of which
end with bright puke
gushing through my fingers.

Her junkie boyfriend's
burnt spoons drooping
like ripe sunflowers.

That tragic,
magic
cake.

The way
my parents' shed
lurches from the weight
of broken old machines.

My God,
it's almost
too sweet.

Killing Spiders

At some point I stopped believing
I stopped taking them outside
or moving them to grass
easier to crush another stupid thing
tell you my brain
is bouncing
through traffic on fire
my arms full of bad electricity
soft hairs
nobody's guitar strings
I spend half my days
wobbling my B-shaped stomach
in mirrors and dark blue windows
thinking it's okay at least I'm good at sex
thinking no it's not okay
I should have muscles
doughy
girl boy
how the word Freak hurts my teeth
how the wild sun moves me to burn
sometimes I can't stop pissing
it's embarrassing
there's a haunted chemistry set
under my belt buckle
I can almost fit my thumb
inside my belly button
sometimes I want to run around town
with my thumb inside my belly button
as if having my thumb

inside my belly button
is magic
I want to tell my psychiatrist
writing poetry makes me feel sick
when I put my fingers down my throat
it's like I'm trying to touch another person
it's like I'm searching for the light switch
the way you look at me
obsessed with clouds
almost everything is a cloud
if it's not a cloud
I don't want to ruin it
with my pill-popping love
my daughter says
they're going to bed
even in the daytime
she says the clouds
are going to bed daddy
I ask her to hug me harder every time
I stand laughing
a manic orchestra
oh my God I miss you
so much my baby
when you're big enough
you will break me
she says pink butterflies
are better than white butterflies
she says flying cars are better
than normal cars
she says mummy daddy
smoke smoke smoke

it feels like my family's worn out
work shoes are piled on my chest
it feels like we should stop
indulging poets who write
as if they're not even breathing
tell them fuck you
you're not even breathing
tell them fuck you
for making me hold my breath
I'm having a panic attack right now
but I'd rather die in a poem
with my balls so tight I'm basically angelic
with my arsehole
sore from shitting bricks in London
with my nipple hair like spiders
with my pink nipples
soft soft soft
I push your hand away because my body
is a Disney princess
colouring book
I fold your mouth into a bloody banknote
as you say shut up you're beautiful
sometimes we fuck as if
it's gonna save the world
with space to dream
of something else
something that'll fill your mouth
with juicy spit
like an American boy
an American girl
America-K-K-K

sometimes I freak myself out
slapping my own bare ass
in the dark
to the beat of the moon
or a drunk
flickering street light
sometimes I pretend I'm a tortoise in Japan
sometimes I pretend to be an indigenous tribe
sometimes I pretend
hell is a frightened father in the wind
when you paint my nails
I think about war
it's the only time I think about war
there's never a wrong time to think about war
and baby
if I kill another spider
that would be like a hundred spiders this week
by the end of the year
there will be a special place for me
in the splendid lore of spiders
I think depression is a cartoon skull
I think everything is a cartoon skull
I think about you thinking about a cartoon skull
and I can breathe
it's like I have always
been
breathing
you understand what this means
I fucking hope so
because
halfway through this poem

my lungs were almost out of credit
and I kept going
the mirrors trembled for my weird shape
they said Killer
they said Oh my God what a beautiful killer
they said Wait for it
wait for it
he's really happening now

Rocket

I stand with the soft, stunned and penniless
parents in the park,
staring at our phones,
over-medicated
with painful lungs
and traumatic childhoods
wondering
what the hell happened.
Drafting messages
explaining everything
to no one in particular.
I pull a face when you call me beautiful
feeling sorry for you
believing such a thing.
It never occurred to me that I might be beautiful.
That anything I did
could ever be described
as beautiful.
The dirty boys made sure of that.
It was my fault: the things they did to me.
I believed this
for such a long time,
didn't tell anyone (lads never do).
Then I went a bit cuckoo.
Girls laughed
and there were clouds
full of small town rain
that smelled like sweaty boys.
So I made friends with blood.

I painted my body with brilliant blood
and begged them all for love.
But boys don't want love.
They worshipped my long hair,
quick to tears, cum-face shivers
through derelict buildings.
When they held me down
I would shriek so loud
hysterical with fear
terrified this meant I enjoyed it
giggling
weak in the dirt.
When you tell me I'm beautiful I promise
to try
to believe you.
They took so much from me
that intimacy
often feels
as if it belongs to them
and we can only borrow it
when we're drunk
out of our minds.
On worse days
I imagine cutting my dick off and tossing it
like a bargain-basement rocket
flashing pink stars
above the factories.
Until I became a man
I thought I must be a girl.
Now I'm supposed to be a man
I often forget

I'm anything at all.
It's easy to forget there is such a thing as beautiful
when we're shivering in the park
worried about our children
losing what we lost.
Sunset in pieces
all around us
like chopped up lifeboats.
I hold my breath
as my daughter disappears
into the silver tunnel
of the big slide, using my sleeve
to wipe away the mud and rain
before she comes out the other side.

Acknowledgements

These poems first appeared in *Asterism Anthology* (Laudanum Press), *Blue of Noon*, *B O D Y*, *Best British Poetry 2015* (Salt), *I Am Not A Silent Poet*, *Poetry Wales*, *Well Versed* (*The Morning Star*), *Your One Phone Call* and *Vanguard Anthology #2*.

Thanks to Chris Crawford, Emily Berry, Jody Porter, Tom Bland, Tiffany Anne Tondut, Ali Lewis, Reuben Woolley, Nia Davies, Richard Skinner, Patrick Davidson Roberts and Martha Sprackland for publishing these poems, and to the Society of Authors for awarding a grant which helped me get started on this book.

Personal thanks to friends and family, of which I am extremely fortunate (and not entirely deserving) to say there are too many to mention. Without your love and support I wouldn't be alive and there would be no poetry.